CW00517536

Alchemy of the Soul: Integrating the Teachings of Imam Ghazali and Modern Psychology for a Happier Life

Ahmad Rahman

Contents

Preface

Imam Ghazali's timeless wisdom and modern psychology's cutting-edge research come together in this ground-breaking book on the secrets of happiness. Drawing on Ghazali's masterpiece, The Alchemy of Happiness, and the latest findings in psychology, this book offers a practical guide to cultivating a fulfilling and joyful life.

Discover the importance of seeking knowledge, building self-discipline, cultivating positive relationships, finding purpose, and meaning, and overcoming obstacles to happiness. With practical steps for incorporating these teachings into daily life, this book is a powerful tool for personal growth and spiritual development.

Whether you're struggling with negative emotions, seeking greater fulfilment in your career and relationships, or simply looking for a deeper understanding of the human psyche, this book is must-read. Join the thousands of readers who have transformed their lives with the wisdom of Imam Ghazali and modern psychology.

Discover how the teachings of Imam Ghazali, a 12th-century Islamic scholar, can transform your life and bring you closer to happiness and fulfilment. In this ground-breaking book, you'll explore the timeless wisdom of Ghazali's masterpiece, The Alchemy of Happiness, and see how it can be applied in a modern context to overcome challenges and achieve your goals. Through Ghazali's teachings, you'll learn the importance of seeking knowledge, cultivating self-discipline, building positive relationships, finding purpose, and meaning, and overcoming obstacles to happiness. You'll also discover how these teachings align with modern psychological research and techniques, making them applicable to anyone seeking a more fulfilling life. Whether you're looking to improve your relationships, advance in your career, or simply find a greater sense of purpose, this book offers practical steps for incorporating Ghazali's teachings into your daily life. You'll gain a deeper understanding of yourself and your place in the world and find the tools you need to live a happier, more fulfilling life. Join the millions of people who have been inspired by Ghazali's teachings for centuries and discover the power of The Alchemy of Happiness in your own life.

Alchemy of the Soul: Integrating the Teachings of Imam Ghazali and Modern Psychology for a Happier Life

Chapter One: Introduction

Imam Ghazali (1058-1111) was a renowned Islamic theologian, philosopher, and mystic from the city of Tus, in present-day Iran. He is widely regarded as one of the most influential Muslim thinkers in history, and his works continue to be studied and debated by scholars and seekers of wisdom across the world.

One of Ghazali's most famous works is the Alchemy of Happiness (Kimiya-yi Sa'adat in Persian), a spiritual treatise that explores the nature of happiness and the path to achieving it. Written in Arabic and completed in 1099, the book draws on Islamic theology, philosophy, and mysticism, as well as Ghazali's personal experiences and insights.

In the Alchemy of Happiness, Ghazali argues that true happiness can only be attained by cultivating a deep and sincere love for God, and by following the teachings of the Quran and the Prophet Muhammad (peace be upon him). He identifies several spiritual obstacles that can hinder one's journey towards happiness, such as ignorance, pride, envy, and attachment to worldly things, and offers practical guidance on how to overcome them.

Throughout the book, Ghazali emphasizes the importance of seeking knowledge, cultivating self-discipline and self-control, building positive relationships with others, and finding purpose and meaning in life. He draws on a rich variety of Islamic sources, including stories from the lives of the prophets and the companions of the Prophet Muhammad, as well as teachings from Sufi masters and other spiritual guides.

The Alchemy of Happiness remains a cherished and widely read book in the Islamic tradition, and its teachings continue to inspire people of all faiths and backgrounds to seek a deeper understanding of happiness and spiritual fulfilment.

The Alchemy of Happiness offers a comprehensive and timeless approach to achieving happiness and spiritual fulfilment that remains relevant today. Many of its teachings have been found to be consistent with modern psychological principles and practices and can provide valuable insights into enhancing well-being and personal growth.

One of the central themes of the book is the importance of self-awareness and self-improvement. Ghazali stresses the need for individuals to identify their negative tendencies and work to overcome them through self-discipline and self-control. This is in line with contemporary psychological theories such as cognitive-behavioural therapy, which emphasizes the importance of self-monitoring and self-regulation in changing behaviour and overcoming negative patterns of thinking.

Another important concept in the book is the idea of purpose and meaning in life. Ghazali argues that true happiness can only be achieved by pursuing a higher purpose and aligning one's actions with the will of God. This is consistent with modern psychological theories of positive psychology, which suggest that individuals who have a sense of purpose and meaning in life are more likely to experience greater happiness and well-being.

Ghazali also emphasizes the importance of positive social connections and relationships. He argues that building strong and supportive relationships with others is essential for achieving happiness and spiritual fulfilment. This is consistent with contemporary psychological research, which has found that social support and positive relationships are crucial for mental and physical health.

Finally, the book emphasizes the importance of mindfulness and reflection in achieving happiness and personal growth. Ghazali encourages individuals to cultivate a deep and sincere awareness of themselves and their surroundings, and to use this awareness to identify their negative tendencies and work to overcome them. This is consistent with modern mindfulness-based approaches to therapy, which have been found to be effective in reducing stress, anxiety, and depression.

Overall, The Alchemy of Happiness offers a rich and nuanced approach to achieving happiness and spiritual fulfilment that remains relevant and insightful today. Its teachings can provide valuable insights into enhancing well-being and personal growth and can inspire individuals to cultivate a deeper sense of self-awareness and purpose in their lives.

The Alchemy of Happiness offers a wealth of wisdom and guidance on how to achieve happiness and spiritual fulfilment in life. Its teachings can be a valuable resource for those seeking to improve their well-being, overcome negative patterns of thinking, and find greater meaning and purpose in life.

One of the keyways in which the book's teachings can be applied to one's life is through self-reflection and self-improvement. Ghazali emphasizes the importance of identifying and overcoming negative tendencies and behaviours, and cultivating positive qualities such as humility, compassion, and gratitude. By practicing self-awareness and self-discipline, individuals can work to transform their inner selves and become more aligned with the teachings of Islam and the pursuit of happiness.

The book's teachings can also be applied to building positive relationships with others. Ghazali stresses the importance of cultivating strong and supportive social connections, and treating others with kindness, respect, and empathy. By practicing these virtues, individuals can enhance their relationships and build a sense of community and belonging.

Another way in which the book's teachings can be applied to one's life is through the pursuit of purpose and meaning. Ghazali argues that true happiness can only be achieved by aligning one's actions with the will of God and pursuing a higher purpose in life. By cultivating a sense of purpose and meaning, individuals can find greater fulfilment and motivation in their daily lives.

Finally, the book's teachings can be applied to mindfulness and self-care. Ghazali encourages individuals to cultivate a deep and sincere awareness of themselves and their surroundings, and to use this awareness to identify their negative tendencies and work to overcome them. By practicing mindfulness and self-care, individuals can reduce stress and anxiety, improve their mental and physical health, and enhance their overall well-being.

Overall, The Alchemy of Happiness offers a rich and profound approach to improving one's life and achieving happiness and spiritual fulfilment. Its teachings can be applied to a wide range of personal and social challenges and can inspire individuals to cultivate a deeper sense of purpose, meaning, and well-being in their lives.

Chapter Two: The Importance of Knowledge

Ghazali places a strong emphasis on the importance of seeking knowledge as a means of achieving spiritual fulfilment. He argues that true happiness and spiritual growth can only be achieved through the pursuit of knowledge and wisdom, and that ignorance and blind adherence to tradition can hinder personal growth and spiritual progress.

In The Alchemy of Happiness, Ghazali encourages individuals to seek knowledge and understanding of the divine and to cultivate a deep and sincere awareness of themselves and their surroundings. He argues that the pursuit of knowledge is essential for developing a strong and authentic relationship with God, and that true knowledge can only be obtained through direct experience and reflection.

Ghazali also stresses the importance of critical thinking and independent inquiry in the pursuit of knowledge. He argues that blind adherence to tradition and authority can lead to a superficial and incomplete understanding of the divine, and that true wisdom can only be attained through rigorous questioning and independent inquiry.

Moreover, Ghazali highlights the role of knowledge in developing moral character and ethical behaviour. He argues that the pursuit of knowledge can help individuals develop virtues such as humility, compassion, and justice, and can guide them towards a more ethical and moral way of life.

Overall, Ghazali's emphasis on seeking knowledge underscores the importance of intellectual curiosity, critical thinking, and personal reflection in the pursuit of spiritual growth and fulfilment. His teachings offer a powerful reminder of the role of knowledge and wisdom in shaping our understanding of the divine, ourselves, and the world around us, and provide a valuable resource for those seeking to deepen their spiritual practice and enhance their personal growth.

Modern psychology has recognized the importance of lifelong learning as a key factor in promoting overall well-being and happiness. Studies have shown that engaging in new learning experiences can help individuals build resilience, enhance their cognitive function, and promote positive emotions and a sense of purpose and meaning in life.

One way in which learning new things can promote well-being is by enhancing cognitive function and brain health. Research has demonstrated that engaging in intellectually stimulating activities, such as learning a new language, playing an instrument, or solving puzzles, can promote brain plasticity and improve cognitive function, memory, and attention.

Learning new things can also promote emotional well-being by providing a sense of accomplishment, satisfaction, and self-efficacy. When individuals engage in new learning experiences and acquire new skills, they can experience a sense of achievement and mastery, which can boost their self-esteem and confidence.

In addition, learning new things can provide a sense of purpose and meaning in life, which is essential for overall well-being. By pursuing new knowledge and skills, individuals can develop a sense of personal growth and fulfilment and feel more connected to their communities and the world around them.

Moreover, learning new things can promote resilience and adaptive coping in the face of stress and adversity. When individuals engage in new learning experiences, they develop new perspectives and strategies for dealing with challenges, which can help them cope more effectively with stress and adversity.

Overall, modern psychology recognizes the importance of lifelong learning as a key factor in promoting overall well-being and happiness. By engaging in new learning experiences and acquiring new knowledge and skills, individuals can enhance their cognitive function, promote emotional well-being, find purpose and meaning in life, and build resilience and adaptive coping strategies.

Incorporating learning into one's life can be a powerful way to promote personal growth and enhance overall well-being. Here are some practical steps for incorporating learning into one's life:

1. Take a class: One of the most effective ways to learn new things is by taking a class. This could be a formal class at a university or community college, or a more informal class offered by a local community centre or online learning platform. Look for classes that cover topics you are interested in or that align with your personal goals.
2. Read a book: Reading is a great way to learn new things and expand your knowledge. Choose books that cover topics you are interested in or that challenge your current understanding of the world. Make it a habit to read for a set amount of time each day or week and set goals for how many books you want to read each year.
3. Watch a documentary: Documentaries are a great way to learn about new topics and gain new perspectives. Choose documentaries that cover topics you are interested in or that challenge your current understanding of the world. Make it a habit to watch one or two documentaries each month and discuss them with friends or family to deepen your understanding of the topic.
4. Attend a workshop or seminar: Workshops and seminars are a great way to learn new skills and gain hands-on experience. Look for workshops or seminars that cover topics you are interested in or that align with your personal goals. Make it a priority to attend at least one workshop or seminar each year.
5. Engage in self-directed learning: Self-directed learning involves setting your own learning goals and pursuing knowledge and skills on your own. This could involve reading books, watching videos, or taking online courses. Set goals for what you want to learn and create a plan for how you will achieve those goals.

By incorporating learning into your life, you can enhance your cognitive function, promote emotional well-being, find purpose and meaning in life, and build resilience and adaptive coping strategies. Choose the learning methods that work best for you and make it a priority to engage in learning on a regular basis.

Chapter Three: The Importance of Self-Discipline and Self-Control

Imam Ghazali's teachings on self-discipline and overcoming the ego's negative impulses are central to his philosophy of spiritual growth and personal transformation. According to Ghazali, the ego, or nafs, is a powerful force that can lead individuals to act on negative impulses and desires, such as greed, anger, and jealousy. To overcome these negative impulses and achieve spiritual fulfilment, Ghazali emphasizes the importance of self-discipline, or Mujahada.

Self-discipline, according to Ghazali, involves a conscious effort to control one's desires and impulses, and to align one's actions with one's higher values and goals. This requires a deep awareness of one's thoughts and feelings, as well as a willingness to challenge and confront one's negative impulses and tendencies.

Ghazali offers several practical strategies for developing self-discipline and overcoming the ego's negative impulses. These include:

1. Mindfulness: Ghazali emphasizes the importance of mindfulness, or self-awareness, in developing self-discipline. By becoming more aware of one's thoughts and feelings, one can identify negative impulses and desires and take steps to control them.

2. Self-reflection: Ghazali also encourages individuals to engage in self-reflection, or Muhasaba, to assess their actions and motives and identify areas for improvement. This involves regularly reflecting on one's thoughts, feelings, and actions, and taking steps to align them with one's higher values and goals.

3. Fasting: Fasting is an important practice in Ghazali's philosophy of self-discipline. By abstaining from food and other pleasures, individuals can learn to control their desires and impulses and develop greater self-control and willpower.
4. Prayer and meditation: Ghazali also emphasize the importance of prayer and meditation in developing self-discipline. By engaging in regular prayer and meditation, individuals can cultivate a sense of inner peace and strength, which can help them resist negative impulses and desires.

In modern psychology, self-discipline is recognized as a key factor in promoting personal growth and success. Studies have shown that individuals with higher levels of self-discipline are better able to control their impulses, set and achieve goals, and cope with stress and adversity.

Overall, Ghazali's teachings on self-discipline and overcoming the ego's negative impulses offer valuable insights for personal growth and spiritual fulfilment. By cultivating self-discipline through mindfulness, self-reflection, fasting, prayer, and meditation, individuals can overcome negative impulses and align their actions with their higher values and goals, promoting personal growth and well-being.

Self-control is a crucial aspect of human psychology that has been extensively studied in modern psychology. Self-control, also known as self-regulation, refers to the ability to control one's thoughts, emotions, and behaviours in order to achieve long-term goals or to adapt to changing environmental demands.

Modern psychology emphasizes the importance of self-control in achieving goals and promoting overall well-being. Research has shown that individuals with higher levels of self-control are more likely to achieve their goals, experience greater life satisfaction, and have better mental and physical health outcomes.

Self-control has been linked to various aspects of human behaviour, including decision-making, impulse control, and emotion regulation. Individuals with higher levels of self-control are better able to resist temptations and impulses that might undermine their long-term goals, and they are more likely to make choices that promote their well-being.

One of the key benefits of self-control is that it helps individuals to delay gratification. Delayed gratification involves the ability to resist immediate rewards in favour of achieving long-term goals. This skill is important in a variety of life domains, from education to health to financial planning.

In addition to delayed gratification, self-control has been linked to other positive outcomes, such as better interpersonal relationships, greater resilience to stress, and improved academic and work performance.

There are several strategies that individuals can use to improve their self-control and promote well-being. These include:

1. Setting clear goals: Setting clear and achievable goals can help individuals to focus their efforts and motivate them to work towards those goals.
2. Building habits: By establishing positive habits, such as regular exercise or healthy eating, individuals can reduce the need for self-control and make it easier to maintain positive behaviours.
3. Practicing mindfulness: Mindfulness practices, such as meditation, can help individuals to develop greater awareness of their thoughts and emotions, which can improve self-control.
4. Seeking social support: Seeking support from others can help individuals to stay motivated and accountable for their goals, which can improve self-control and increase the likelihood of success.

In conclusion, modern psychology recognizes the importance of self-control in achieving goals and promoting overall well-being. By developing self-control through setting clear goals, building habits, practicing mindfulness, and seeking social support, individuals can improve their ability to resist impulses and achieve long-term success.

Building self-discipline is a process that requires conscious effort and dedication. Here are some practical steps that individuals can take to build self-discipline:

1. Identify areas of weakness: The first step in building self-discipline is to identify areas of weakness. This might include unhealthy habits, procrastination, or lack of focus. By identifying these areas, individuals can begin to understand the triggers that lead to self-indulgence and take steps to overcome them.

2. Set clear goals: Once individuals have identified areas of weakness, they can set clear goals to overcome them. For example, if the weakness is procrastination, the goal might be to complete a specific task within a certain timeframe. Setting clear and achievable goals can help individuals to focus their efforts and motivate them to work towards those goals.

3. Create a plan: Once goals have been set, individuals can create a plan to achieve them. This might involve breaking down larger goals into smaller, more manageable tasks, or creating a schedule to ensure that tasks are completed on time. Having a plan in place can help individuals to stay focused and avoid distractions.

4. Practice mindfulness: Mindfulness practices, such as meditation, can help individuals to develop greater awareness of their thoughts and emotions. This can help to improve self-control and increase the ability to resist impulses.

5. Reward progress: Rewarding progress can help to reinforce positive behaviours and encourage continued self-discipline. Rewards might include taking time for self-care activities or treating oneself to a small indulgence after achieving a goal.

6. Seek support: Seeking support from friends, family, or a therapist can be helpful in building self-discipline. Support can help to provide accountability and encouragement and can help individuals to stay motivated.

Overall, building self-discipline is a process that requires patience, dedication, and a willingness to change. By identifying areas of weakness, setting clear goals, creating a plan, practicing mindfulness, rewarding progress, and seeking support, individuals can develop greater self-discipline and achieve their goals.

Chapter Four: The Importance of Love and Social Connections

One of the key teachings of Imam Ghazali in "The Alchemy of Happiness" is the importance of cultivating love for God and others as a means of achieving true happiness. According to Ghazali, human beings have an innate longing for love and connection, and this longing can only be fulfilled through love for God and others.

Ghazali believed that love for God is the foundation of all other forms of love, and that it is only through this love that individuals can experience true happiness and fulfilment. He saw love for God as a transformative force that could change individuals from within, leading to a greater sense of purpose and meaning in life.

In addition to love for God, Ghazali also emphasized the importance of cultivating love for others. He believed that love for others is a natural extension of love for God, and that it is through acts of kindness and compassion towards others that individuals can experience true happiness.

Ghazali's teachings on love and happiness are relevant to modern psychology in that research has shown that social connections and positive relationships are key factors in promoting well-being and happiness. Studies have found that individuals who have strong social connections and positive relationships tend to experience less stress, better physical health, and greater life satisfaction.

Practical steps for cultivating love for God and others might include engaging in spiritual practices such as prayer, meditation, or reading religious texts, volunteering in the community, or trying to connect with others in meaningful ways.

In summary, Ghazali's teachings on cultivating love for God and others highlight the importance of social connections and spiritual fulfilment in achieving true happiness. By incorporating these teachings into one's life, individuals can experience greater meaning and purpose, and build stronger relationships with others.

Modern psychology has extensively researched the importance of positive relationships for well-being, and the findings have consistently shown that social connections and positive relationships are key factors in promoting overall health and happiness.

Studies have shown that individuals who have strong social support networks tend to have better mental health outcomes, lower levels of stress and anxiety, and greater life satisfaction. Positive relationships can also promote physical health, as individuals with strong social connections are more likely to engage in healthy behaviours and have a lower risk of chronic diseases.

Moreover, positive relationships can provide individuals with a sense of purpose and meaning and can contribute to a greater sense of self-worth and self-esteem. This, in turn, can lead to greater confidence and resilience in the face of challenges.

In addition to the positive effects of social support and positive relationships on individual well-being, research has also shown that strong social connections can have a positive impact on society. Communities with strong social connections tend to have lower crime rates, better economic outcomes, and greater social cohesion.

Overall, modern psychology recognizes the crucial role that positive relationships play in promoting well-being and emphasizes the importance of cultivating and maintaining strong social connections. This can be achieved through a variety of means, such as building relationships with family and friends, participating in social activities or clubs, and volunteering in the community.

Building positive relationships is an important aspect of promoting overall well-being. Here are some practical steps for building positive relationships:

1. Spend time with loved ones: Make time to connect with family and friends on a regular basis. This can include scheduling weekly dinners, game nights, or outings together.
2. Join a social club: Joining a social club or organization can provide opportunities to meet new people with similar interests. This can include joining a sports team, book club, or hobby group.
3. Volunteer in the community: Volunteering in the community can provide a sense of purpose and fulfilment, while also allowing for opportunities to meet new people and build positive relationships.
4. Attend social events: Attend social events, such as parties, networking events, or community gatherings. This can provide opportunities to meet new people and build positive connections.
5. Practice active listening: When connecting with others, practice active listening by giving them your full attention, asking questions, and engaging in genuine conversation.
6. Show gratitude: Express gratitude towards others by thanking them for their support, expressing appreciation for their presence in your life, and offering words of encouragement and support.
7. Be authentic: Building positive relationships requires authenticity and vulnerability. Be willing to share your thoughts, feelings, and experiences with others, and encourage them to do the same.

Overall, building positive relationships requires intentionality and effort, but the benefits to overall well-being are worth it. By trying to connect with others in meaningful ways, individuals can experience greater happiness, fulfilment, and purpose in their lives.

Chapter Five: Finding Purpose and Meaning

Imam Ghazali's teachings emphasize the importance of preparing for the afterlife in this life. According to Ghazali, the purpose of life is to prepare for the eternal life to come, and this can be achieved through a variety of means, including practicing good deeds, seeking knowledge, and purifying the soul.

Ghazali believed that individuals should live their lives with the understanding that death is imminent and that the afterlife is a reality. He believed that the only way to ensure a positive outcome in the afterlife is to lead a righteous life in this world. Ghazali taught that individuals should strive to cultivate a strong connection with God, to perform good deeds, and to avoid sins and immoral behaviour.

Ghazali also emphasized the importance of purifying the soul, as he believed that the soul is the foundation of one's relationship with God. According to Ghazali, purifying the soul involves controlling one's ego and desires, cultivating positive character traits, and seeking spiritual growth through acts of worship and devotion.

While Ghazali's teachings on the afterlife may differ from modern psychology, there are some similarities in the emphasis on the importance of living a purposeful life and preparing for the future. In modern psychology, the concept of "meaning making" involves finding purpose and meaning in one's life, and this has been shown to contribute to greater well-being and resilience.

Overall, Ghazali's teachings on the afterlife emphasize the importance of living a righteous and purposeful life and provide guidance on how to prepare for the eternal life to come. By focusing on the afterlife, Ghazali's teachings encourage individuals to prioritize their spiritual growth and to strive for a higher purpose, which can contribute to greater fulfilment and well-being in this life as well.

Modern psychology recognizes the importance of having a sense of purpose and meaning in life. Research has shown that individuals who have a clear sense of purpose tend to experience greater well-being, resilience, and satisfaction with life. In fact, having a sense of purpose has been found to be a key predictor of mental and physical health outcomes.

Having a sense of purpose involves feeling that one's life has direction and meaning, and that one's actions are contributing to a larger goal or purpose. This can involve a variety of factors, including a sense of fulfilment in one's work or relationships, a connection to one's community or society, or a belief in a higher power or spiritual purpose.

There are many benefits to having a sense of purpose in life. For example, individuals with a clear sense of purpose tend to have greater motivation and resilience in the face of challenges or setbacks. They also tend to experience less stress and anxiety and may have lower rates of depression and other mental health problems.

There are many ways to cultivate a sense of purpose and meaning in life. This can involve setting goals and working towards them, pursuing activities that align with one's values and passions, or engaging in meaningful relationships or social causes. Additionally, practices such as mindfulness meditation and gratitude can help individuals develop a greater sense of purpose and meaning in their daily lives.

Overall, modern psychology recognizes the importance of having a sense of purpose and meaning in life and provides many tools and strategies for individuals to cultivate this sense of purpose in their daily lives. By prioritizing purpose and meaning, individuals can experience greater well-being, satisfaction, and fulfilment in their lives.

Finding purpose and meaning in life is a personal journey that requires self-reflection, exploration, and action. Here are some practical steps that can help individuals find and pursue their sense of purpose and meaning:

1. Reflect on values and goals: Take some time to reflect on what matters most in life, and what values are most important to you. Ask yourself questions such as: What kind of person do I want to be? What kind of impact do I want to have in the world? What are my long-term goals and aspirations? Use this reflection to identify your core values and goals.

2. Identify passions and strengths: Consider what activities or experiences bring you the most joy and fulfilment, and what you are naturally good at. Identify your passions and strengths and think about how you can use them to contribute to a larger goal or purpose.

3. Explore opportunities: Explore opportunities for pursuing your passions and goals, such as joining a club or organization, volunteering, or taking a class. Look for ways to align your passions and strengths with meaningful activities that contribute to a larger purpose.

4. Set goals and act: Set specific, measurable goals that align with your values and passions, and take action towards achieving them. This may involve breaking down larger goals into smaller, more manageable steps, or seeking out support and resources to help you achieve your goals.

5. Practice mindfulness and gratitude: Incorporate practices such as mindfulness meditation and gratitude into your daily routine. These practices can help you stay focused on the present moment, cultivate a greater sense of purpose and meaning, and stay motivated in the pursuit of your goals.

By taking these practical steps, individuals can begin to cultivate a greater sense of purpose and meaning in their lives. With a clear sense of purpose, individuals can experience greater well-being, satisfaction, and fulfilment in all areas of their lives.

Chapter Six: Overcoming Obstacles to Happiness

Imam Ghazali recognized that there are many obstacles that can prevent individuals from experiencing true happiness, including anxiety, envy, and attachment to worldly things. In his book, "The Alchemy of Happiness," he provides practical guidance on how to overcome these obstacles and cultivate a greater sense of inner peace and contentment.

Anxiety: Ghazali teaches that anxiety is often the result of excessive worry about the future or regret about the past. He encourages individuals to practice mindfulness and focus on the present moment, as well as to trust in God's plan and surrender control over things that are beyond their control.

Envy: Ghazali believes that envy is a toxic emotion that can prevent individuals from experiencing true happiness. He advises individuals to focus on their own blessings and avoid comparing themselves to others, as well as to cultivate a sense of gratitude for what they have.

Attachment to worldly things: According to Ghazali, attachment to worldly things can prevent individuals from experiencing true happiness, as it creates a constant sense of longing and dissatisfaction. He encourages individuals to cultivate detachment and focus on the eternal, rather than the temporary, aspects of life.

To apply these teachings to modern psychology, research has shown that anxiety, envy, and attachment to worldly things can all have negative effects on mental health and well-being. Mindfulness and gratitude practices have been shown to be effective in reducing anxiety and promoting well-being, while avoiding social comparison and focusing on gratitude can help reduce envy. Cultivating detachment and focusing on the eternal aspects of life can also help reduce attachment to material possessions and increase overall well-being.

To apply these teachings in daily life, individuals can practice mindfulness and gratitude, focus on their own blessings rather than comparing themselves to others, and prioritize spiritual practices such as prayer or meditation. They can also work on cultivating detachment from material possessions and focusing on their eternal values and goals. By doing so, individuals can overcome the obstacles to happiness and cultivate a greater sense of inner peace and contentment.

In addition to the obstacles mentioned above, Ghazali also discusses other hindrances to happiness, such as pride, anger, and greed. He advises individuals to practice humility, patience, and generosity to overcome these negative traits and cultivate positive ones instead.

Pride: Ghazali teaches that pride can be a major obstacle to happiness, as it creates a sense of superiority that can lead to isolation and arrogance. He encourages individuals to practice humility and recognize that all humans are equal in the eyes of God.

Anger: According to Ghazali, anger is often the result of unmet expectations and can lead to destructive behaviour and strained relationships. He advises individuals to practice patience and forgiveness, as well as to channel their anger into productive activities.

Greed: Ghazali believes that greed is a major hindrance to happiness, as it creates a constant sense of desire and can lead to selfish behaviour. He encourages individuals to practice generosity and give to those in need, as well as to recognize that true wealth comes from spiritual and moral virtues, rather than material possessions.

Modern psychology also recognizes the negative effects of pride, anger, and greed on mental health and well-being. Practicing humility, patience, forgiveness, and generosity have all been shown to have positive effects on mental health, including reducing stress and promoting positive relationships.

To apply these teachings in daily life, individuals can practice humility by recognizing their limitations and treating others with respect and kindness. They can practice patience and forgiveness by refraining from reacting impulsively to stressful situations and learning to let go of grudges. They can practice generosity by giving to those in need and recognizing that true wealth comes from spiritual and moral virtues, rather than material possessions.

In conclusion, Imam Ghazali's teachings in "The Alchemy of Happiness" offer practical guidance on how to overcome obstacles to happiness and cultivate a greater sense of inner peace and contentment. By incorporating these teachings into our daily lives and combining them with modern psychological practices, we can work towards achieving a more fulfilling and meaningful existence.

Modern psychology recognizes the importance of coping with negative emotions and thoughts in order to promote mental health and well-being. There are several evidence-based strategies that individuals can use to cope with negative emotions and thoughts.

One effective coping strategy is cognitive-behavioural therapy (CBT). CBT helps individuals identify and change negative thought patterns that contribute to negative emotions. It teaches individuals to recognize when negative thoughts are occurring, evaluate their accuracy and helpfulness, and replace them with more positive and realistic thoughts.

Another effective coping strategy is mindfulness-based interventions. Mindfulness involves paying attention to the present moment with a non-judgmental attitude. This can be practiced through techniques such as meditation, deep breathing, and body scans. Mindfulness-based interventions have been shown to be effective in reducing symptoms of anxiety and depression and improving overall well-being.

Additionally, building positive relationships and engaging in enjoyable activities can also be effective coping strategies. Having a support system can provide individuals with emotional support and help them to cope with negative emotions. Engaging in activities that bring joy and pleasure can also help to boost mood and provide a sense of fulfilment.

Overall, modern psychology emphasizes the importance of developing effective coping strategies to manage negative emotions and thoughts. By incorporating evidence-based practices such as CBT, mindfulness, and building positive relationships into daily life, individuals can work towards achieving greater emotional regulation and overall well-being.

here are some practical steps that can be taken to overcome obstacles to happiness, such as anxiety, envy, and attachment to worldly things:

1. Mindfulness practice: Incorporating mindfulness practice into daily life can help individuals to become more aware of their thoughts and emotions and develop greater emotional regulation. This can involve techniques such as deep breathing, body scans, and meditation. Apps such as Headspace and Calm can provide guidance and support for developing a regular mindfulness practice.

2. Cognitive-behavioural therapy (CBT): CBT can help individuals identify and change negative thought patterns that contribute to negative emotions. Techniques such as cognitive restructuring, thought challenging, and behavioural activation can be effective in reducing symptoms of anxiety and depression. CBT can be practiced with the help of a mental health professional, or through online resources such as MoodGYM and CBT Online.

3. Seeking professional help: If individuals are struggling with persistent negative emotions or thoughts, seeking professional help can be an effective step towards overcoming obstacles to happiness. This can involve seeing a therapist or counsellor, or consulting with a healthcare provider to explore medication options if needed.

4. Cultivating positive relationships: Building positive relationships with friends, family, and community members can provide individuals with emotional support and help them

to cope with negative emotions. This can involve engaging in social activities, joining a community group or club, or volunteering in the community.

5. Engaging in enjoyable activities: Engaging in activities that bring joy and pleasure can help to boost mood and provide a sense of fulfilment. This can involve hobbies, exercise, creative pursuits, or simply spending time in nature.

By incorporating these practical steps into daily life, individuals can work towards overcoming obstacles to happiness and achieving greater well-being.

Chapter Seven: Applying the Teachings to Daily Life

Here are some practical steps for incorporating the teachings of Imam Ghazali and modern psychology into daily life:

1. Seek knowledge: Incorporate regular learning into your routine by taking a class, reading a book, or watching a documentary. Reflect on what you have learned and how it can be applied to your life.
2. Practice self-discipline: Identify areas of weakness and plan to overcome them. Set goals and hold yourself accountable. Engage in practices such as mindfulness, meditation, or prayer to develop greater self-awareness and self-control.
3. Cultivate positive relationships: Spend time with loved ones, join a social club, or volunteer in the community. Practice empathy and compassion in your interactions with others.
4. Find purpose and meaning: Reflect on your values and goals and plan to pursue them. Set aside time each day for activities that align with your values and bring a sense of purpose to your life.
5. Overcome obstacles to happiness: Practice mindfulness, cognitive-behavioural therapy techniques, or seek professional help if needed to overcome negative emotions and thoughts. Engage in enjoyable activities that bring joy and pleasure to your life.

By incorporating these practical steps into daily life, individuals can integrate the teachings of Imam Ghazali and modern psychology into their lives and work towards achieving greater well-being and fulfilment.

Here are some examples of how the teachings of Imam Ghazali and modern psychology can be applied to various aspects of life:

1. Work: Incorporating the teachings of self-discipline and purpose can be especially beneficial in the context of work. By setting goals and holding oneself accountable, one can stay focused and motivated towards achieving professional success. Practicing mindfulness and engaging in enjoyable activities outside of work can also help reduce stress and improve work-life balance.

2. Relationships: Cultivating positive relationships is essential to overall well-being. By practicing empathy and compassion, individuals can strengthen their relationships with loved ones and friends. Regularly engaging in activities with others, such as volunteering or joining a social club, can also help build and maintain positive relationships.

3. Personal growth: Incorporating the teachings of seeking knowledge and overcoming obstacles can be especially helpful in achieving personal growth. By regularly learning and reflecting on one's own values and goals, individuals can work towards greater self-awareness and self-improvement. Practicing mindfulness and cognitive-behavioural therapy techniques can also help overcome obstacles to personal growth, such as anxiety or negative thought patterns.

Overall, by incorporating the teachings of Imam Ghazali and modern psychology into various aspects of life, individuals can work towards achieving greater well-being and fulfilment in all areas of their lives.

To the readers out there, I want to encourage you to take small steps towards incorporating the teachings of Imam Ghazali and modern psychology into your life. It's important to remember that personal growth is a journey, and it doesn't happen overnight. By taking small steps towards implementing these teachings, you can gradually work towards greater well-being and fulfilment.

Remember to celebrate your progress along the way, no matter how small it may seem. Every step you take towards greater self-awareness and self-improvement is a step in the right direction.

Whether it's taking a class to learn something new, practicing mindfulness, or strengthening a relationship with a loved one, each small step can make a big difference in your overall well-being.

So don't be discouraged if you don't see immediate results. Keep taking small steps towards implementing these teachings and remember to celebrate your progress along the way. With time and effort, you can work towards achieving greater happiness and fulfilment in your life.

Chapter Eight: Conclusion

In summary, Imam Ghazali's "Alchemy of Happiness" teaches that true happiness and fulfilment can only be achieved through a deep spiritual connection with God. This connection is cultivated through seeking knowledge, self-discipline, love for God and others, preparing for the afterlife, and overcoming negative emotions and thoughts.

These teachings are relevant to modern psychology in that they emphasize the importance of continuous learning, building self-discipline, cultivating positive relationships, finding purpose, and meaning in life, and coping with negative emotions. By incorporating these teachings into daily life, individuals can work towards greater well-being and fulfilment.

Practical steps for implementing these teachings include taking a class, reflecting on values and goals, spending time with loved ones, practicing mindfulness, seeking professional help if needed, and celebrating small steps towards personal growth. Overall, the teachings of "Alchemy of Happiness" and modern psychology can contribute to a happier and more fulfilling life by providing a framework for spiritual and personal development.

I encourage readers to continue exploring the teachings of Imam Ghazali and modern psychology and to make them a part of their daily lives. While implementing these teachings may require effort and patience, the rewards of a more fulfilling and spiritually connected life are worth it.

By seeking knowledge, building self-discipline, cultivating positive relationships, finding purpose, and meaning, and overcoming negative emotions, individuals can work towards a more holistic approach to well-being. It is important to remember that progress takes time and effort, but by taking small steps towards personal growth and celebrating each achievement, individuals can continue the path towards a more fulfilling life.

Ultimately, the teachings of "Alchemy of Happiness" and modern psychology offer valuable insights into how individuals can lead happier and more fulfilling lives. By incorporating these teachings into our daily lives, we can cultivate a greater sense of purpose, connection, and well-being.

Absolutely! Here are some resources for further learning and support:

1. "The Alchemy of Happiness" by Imam Ghazali - the original text that provides in-depth teachings on spiritual and psychological growth.
2. "The Power of Now" by Eckhart Tolle - a modern book that explores the importance of mindfulness and living in the present moment.
3. "The Four Agreements" by Don Miguel Ruiz - a book that offers practical guidance on how to overcome self-limiting beliefs and cultivate positive relationships.
4. "Mindfulness: An Eight-Week Plan for Finding Peace in a Frantic World" by Mark Williams and Danny Penman - a step-by-step guide to mindfulness practices that can help reduce stress and improve well-being.
5. Psychology Today - an online publication that offers articles and resources on a wide range of topics related to psychology and personal growth.
6. Meetup - a website that allows individuals to join local groups based on shared interests and goals, including groups focused on spirituality and personal growth.
7. Spiritual Centres - many cities and towns have spiritual centres or groups that offer resources and support for individuals interested in personal growth and spiritual development. Some examples include Unity, Science of Mind, and Centres for Spiritual Living.

I hope these resources are helpful in continuing the journey towards personal growth and well-being!

It has been an honour to share with you the teachings of Imam Ghazali and their relevance to modern psychology. I hope that the ideas and practical steps we have explored in this book will inspire you to cultivate a happier and more fulfilling life.

Remember that implementing change takes time and effort, but small steps can lead to great progress. Celebrate each step forward, no matter how small, and be patient with yourself as you continue your journey.

If you find yourself in need of further support, know that there are many resources available to you, including books, websites, and local groups that focus on spiritual and psychological growth. Never hesitate to reach out and seek help when you need it.

Thank you for taking the time to read this book and explore these teachings with me. I wish you all the best in your pursuit of happiness and fulfilment.

Printed in Great Britain
by Amazon

25746903R00030